Flash Tales

by

Joan Sikes,
Diane Neal
Janda Raker, editor
Dianne G. Sagan
Mary Barbara Gendusa-Yokum

Flash Tales
Copyright 2010
by
Joan Sikes, editor
Diane Neal
Janda Raker
Dianne G. Sagan
Mary Barbara Gendusa-Yokum
ISBN 978-1-934335-37-6
ISBN 1-934335-37-1

One Night Books #12

WordWright.biz, Inc.
WordWright Business Park
46561 State Highway 118
Alpine, TX 79830

Printed in the United States of America

Enjoy!

Joan Sikes

Our Dedications

From Joan Sikes:
   To my husband, John, who, when seeing me engrossed at the computer, will tiptoe out of the room.

From Diane Neal:
   To Herschel, my husband, and my sons Herschel III and Terry and their families, and my son Jarrod, my editor.

From Janda Raker:
   To Lyle, for all his encouragement.

From Dianne G. Sagan:
   To my husband, Greg, who encourages me whether I write short or long.

From Mary Barbara Gendusa-Yokum:
   To my children Jeff and Kristin and my grandchildren for their constant love and enthusiastic support.

From all the authors:
   We further dedicate this book to all writers and to everyone who takes the Flash Fiction challenge.

Introduction

If you love to read but find yourself short of time, with only a minute now and then, such as during breaks at work, at your children's ball games, while preparing meals, on a commuter train, while waiting for a friend, during television commercials, you can pick up this book and read, in just one minute, a complete story!

Flash fiction is extremely short fiction, length decided by the author or editor. Some editors limit stories to as short as fifty-five words, some are as long as two thousand, and each must include all the elements of a complete story: setting, characters, conflict, and resolution. A flash-fiction story by Ernest Hemingway is famous as being the shortest complete story. He used only six words.

Our small writers group of five members meets every week to critique each other's work. Included are award-winning writers, nationally published authors, even one ghost writer. Among the five of us, we have written memoirs, travel essays, thrillers, poetry, personal interviews, devotionals, humor, and short stories. But not long ago, we had trouble getting motivated.

We had heard of flash fiction, and some of us had attended a workshop on how to write it. One member of our group suggested each of us write a flash fiction story every week, and proposed a plan for getting started.

Every Tuesday when we gathered, each of us wrote down a word—any word. We shared our words, and everyone went home to write a story using all of them in some form. The group decided on a one hundred words limit, plus the title. The next week, we reconvened and read our tales aloud. Good stuff! At the end of a year, every one of us had written forty stories, in many different genres. We critiqued them, polished them, and this book is the result. We have included one hundred stories, with another hundred to follow in another volume.

Sometimes you, the reader, will feel that one of the words used was not the best choice for that concept. Please keep in mind that we were "required" to use certain words and create the story around them. I originally thought, especially because we are all women and not too far apart in age, that surely everyone would write the same basic story for a set of words. Quite the contrary. This exercise proved that we're all different.

These stories served their original purpose and got us writing again. However, we all reaped an unexpected benefit. We learned to write without wasted words. Creating flash fiction has improved everything we write.

Then our group realized other writers could benefit from this exercise by reading these tales and learning from our experience. And don't almost all readers really wish to write? So this book is also for you, the reader-writers among us.

If our idea appeals to you, feel free to write your own stories using our word lists. Or, you could gather a group of friends and adopt our format. If you'd like to share any of your tales with us, send them to me at JandaRaker@gmail.com. Perhaps we can compile another book and include your stories.

All our word lists are in the back of the book, as well as the relevant five words at the beginning of each group of stories.

We think you'll most enjoy reading these when you can see the lists of words that inspired those tales and when you can compare the different tales based on each word list. So in every group are five stories, one each by Diane Neal, Dianne Sagan, me (the editor/compiler, Janda Raker), Joan Sikes, and Mary Gendusa Yokum. You may notice that a few of the lists contain six words rather than five. A sixth member of our group, Cindy Rios, chose not to join us in this publication, but we recognize he contributions as an outstanding writer who inspired us all.

So, we're sharing these stories with you, and we hope you enjoy them. If you have a minute, jump in and read a story.

From all of us,
Wanda Raker
Diane Neal
Dianne Sagan
Joan Sikes
Mary Barbara Gendusa-Yokum

#1 Flash Tales
(lantern, fur, cabbage, embellish, scratch)

The Walrus Speaks
(Neal)

The <u>fur</u> cowl on the black wool dress did little to soften or <u>embellish</u> the features of the <u>lantern</u>-jawed woman. Her entrance into the classroom of Charles Dodgson pierced the atmosphere like a knife.

"What are you doing?" she asked him.

"I am writing a poem for children," he replied.

She looked at the paper in front of him and read aloud:

"'The time has come,' the Walrus said,

'To talk of many things: Of shoes and ships and sealing-wax, of <u>cabbages</u> and kings.'"

"You call this a poem? It doesn't seem quite up to <u>scratch</u>."

Silenced
(Sagan)

The moonless night shrouded two soldiers who crept through <u>cabbage</u> fields to a ramshackle house. They knew their battalion's survival depended on them. Military Intelligence reports said no one lived there after the bombing raid.

A noise, like fingernails <u>scratching</u> wood. The men froze.

One <u>fur</u>-clad man whispered, "I thought it was empty."

The other signaled agreement.

An <u>embellished</u> intelligence report gave them false security. The trap closed.

Suddenly, a <u>lantern</u> cast an eerie glow across the exposed crouching intruders. Shots rang out. Two soldiers lay face up with eyes that could not see. Another incursion stopped.

Trick or Treat
(Raker)

On the porch, behind the jack-o'-<u>lantern</u>, sat a lifelike black cat, <u>fur</u> sticking out in all directions. Its puffy, round face resembled a <u>Cabbage</u>-Patch doll. An orange collar <u>embellished</u> with gleaming studs adorned its neck.

A miniature Dracula, complete with red-satin-lined cape, trod hesitantly up the sidewalk. His father waited at the curb, encouraging. "It's okay. He's not real. Go on up and ring the doorbell."

As the little hand reached for the button, the cat leaped on the young goblin, its claws <u>scratching</u> his face.

The youngster ran down the road screaming, "Daddy, you lied!"

Backfire
(Sikes)

Dorene dropped the shredded <u>cabbage</u> into the soup and thought of her kitchen back home. Who would've thought I'd ever prepare a meal from <u>scratch</u>? And by the light of a kerosene <u>lantern</u>.

Later, while resting on the <u>fur</u> rug by the fire and rubbing her full stomach, she chuckled about Chuck's predicament. And *he* had wanted *her* to taste primitive living.

She sighed and mused. "I hope Search and Rescue finds him before he succumbs to hypothermia. I'm planning to get a lot of mileage out of this story — and with <u>embellishments</u>."

Ball of Fur
(Gendusa-Yokum)

One evening I heard a strange sound coming from outside — <u>scratch</u>, scratch, scratch. I looked through my window blinds, and by the light from my porch <u>lantern</u>, I could see a brown <u>fur</u> ball hopping among the <u>cabbages</u>. I was so afraid my parents would notice and try to trap the bunny. They love homemade rabbit stew. I decided to turn on soft music as a perfect cover-up for the unusual sounds.

The next day at school, I <u>embellished</u> what happened. "Guess what! Last night I saw a bunny in my garden carrying a basket filled with colored Easter eggs."

Now You Try!
(lantern, fur, cabbage, embellish, scratch)

_____

_____

_____

_____

_____

_____

_____

_____

_____

_____

_____

_____

_____

_____

_____

_____

_____

_____

_____

_____

_____

_____

#2 Flash Tales
(spine, jute, exfoliate, travel, ocean, battery)

The Beauty Battalion
(Neal)

Ethel sat Indian-style on her <u>jute</u> area rug and watched her favorite episode of *Designing Women* on TV. Anthony had hurt his back working at Suzanne's house. Fearing for his <u>spine</u>, she installed him in a frou-frou bedroom. She called in a <u>battery</u> of technicians and subjected her prisoner to various beauty treatments.

Terrified by their <u>oceanic</u> onslaught, he escaped under cover of night, <u>traveling</u> to Julia's house on his hands and knees.

Piteously, he cried out, "Help me. Suzanne's called in a whole troop of experts for tomorrow." Eyes bulging in terror, he squealed, "They're gonna <u>exfoliate</u> me!"

Sea-Spa Holiday
(Sagan)

Joanne deserved a break from her meetings and <u>travel</u>—career mainstays. She left corporate America behind for a spa vacation, the first time in five years, but sure she could get away. Personal sacrifice and professional diligence made her one of the first female CEOs of a Fortune 500 company. She luxuriated in a massage for her aching muscles and kinked <u>spine</u>. She savored the exfoliating mask and relaxed into a jute hammock. She listened to the ocean waves and unconsciously dialed the office from habit. The phone couldn't connect. Her assistant had confiscated the cell phone battery.

Lars
(Raker)

Lars loved to travel. Even when the cruise ship sank, he was exhilarated to find himself alone on a tiny desert island. With a life raft and some tools, he knew he could survive, though the mainland was hundreds of miles away.

He gathered fruits and nuts. He harvested jute for fishing line. Palm leaves roofed a shelter. But finally he'd exfoliated the entire island. Only barren spines of plants remained.

Lars packed his belongings and slipped his boat between ocean waves. The trolling motor started. He was optimistic. Hopefully the battery wouldn't run down.

Waiting Room Decision
(Sikes)

Travel, the advertisement read. Megan grimaced. *Sure. How? When?* She forced the flyer between her novel's pages, grasped the spine, and slammed it shut.

Megan shouted across the waiting room, "How long does it take to install a battery, anyway?"

"I'll check," the attendant answered.

I'll never make that meeting. Relax, Megan.

6

A plant swinging in a <u>jute</u> sling mesmerized her. It became a ship cruising on the <u>ocean</u>.

No deadlines, no conferences . . . Well, why not? Like bark <u>exfoliating</u> from a diseased tree, all reticence fell away.

She withdrew the travel folder and pulled out her cell phone.

Crude and Rude
(Gendusa-Yokum)

Louisa shuddered at the manager's presence. Such a <u>spineless</u> creep, Mr. Woldruff would be an embarrassment even to be counted among the invertebrates. At least when they <u>exfoliate,</u> they do so to become new beings adapting to their surroundings.

His brash character reminds me of shredded <u>jute</u> with its harsh fibers grating and irritating to everyone around, she thought. *When I am near such a fault-finding person, I fantasize <u>traveling</u> across the <u>ocean</u> to be as far away as possible.*

"Marcus, remind me to get a new <u>battery</u>. If he comes close, I might light a spark to frighten him away."

Now You Try!
(spine, jute, exfoliate, travel, ocean, battery)

_____

_____

_____

_____

_____

_____

_____

_____

_____

_____

_____

_____

_____

_____

_____

_____

_____

_____

_____

_____

_____

_____

_____

_____

_____

#3 Flash Tales
(stagger, gastric, turkey, diamond, chimney)

Diamonds Are a Girl's Best Friend
(Neal)

Brittany checked the chimney vent before starting a fire. She wore a tasteful, low-cut black dress in anticipation of a romantic dinner with her husband. Humming as she placed the centerpiece of lilies and roses on the table, she glanced up at the tall case clock. She turned, smiling, as she heard Russ at the door. He entered, staggering again with a drunken grin on his face. Brittany's gastric juices churned.

Why did I marry this turkey? she thought. The diamond ring on her finger twinkled at her. Oh. That's why.

Near Tragedy
(Sagan)

The maid staggered into the conservatory coughing. "A fire in the kitchen chimney!" She gasped and fainted at the butler's feet. He knelt to her aid.

Around them, well-dressed women ignored the scene, flaunting diamonds while sipping champagne, enjoying cucumber-and-turkey hors d'oeuvres.

The hostess, Mrs. Hampton, pushed the servants out of sight as her gastric acid churned. "Back to the kitchen." She smelled smoke. Her hand went to her throat. "Oh, no!"

The butler called 911 and escorted guests to safety in

the gardens, holding a tray of champagne in one hand and the maid in the other.

Holiday Blues
(Raker)

Byron had always loved Julia. Reunited after fifty years, he still felt the spark.

But Byron was becoming absent-minded. He rented a costume, ideal for the holiday. <u>Diamond</u> ring nestling in his pocket under the padded abdomen, he ascended the roof apparently without Julia hearing him.

Wiggling down the <u>chimney</u>, head first, he felt <u>gastric</u> juices lodge in his throat. He floundered through the ashes, got to his feet, and <u>staggered</u> across the room. Julia entered.

He spied the decorated tree just as her scornful voice pierced his heart.

"No, Byron. Not a <u>turkey</u> suit, a Santa Claus suit!"

Unexpected Wages
(Sikes)

Luke watched Virgil <u>stagger</u> through the door and muttered, "That <u>turkey</u>, why can't he fix his own <u>chimney</u>?" He downed another swallow of beer, hoping to calm his <u>gastric</u> juices, then reluctantly followed Virgil.

Luke surveyed the damage. He removed a loose brick, scraped off some mortar, then struggled to replace it. It wouldn't fit. He thrust his hand into the opening and retrieved the offending object. "No wonder. This rock was in the way," he said. But upon closer observation, he realized it was no ordinary rock, but an enormous <u>diamond</u>.

Luke whistled as he worked.

Finders Keepers
(Gendusa-Yokum)

Sammy came running in. "Ma, something is wrong with my <u>turkey</u>, Petey. He's <u>staggering</u> all over the yard. Hurry, we've got to help him. Can we call the veterinarian?"

"Where is he, Sammy? I don't see him!"

"He went that way. I can see his tail. Oh, no, he just bumped into the <u>chimney</u>. Look, Mama!"

"Sammy, he looks pretty bad. His feathers are all ruffled. He's choking like he has <u>gastric</u> problems. Wait, what's that shining over there? A <u>diamond</u> ring! This must be what old Mrs. Carlson was looking for last week. And no one believed her."

Now You Try!
(stagger, gastric, turkey, diamond, chimney)

_____

_____

_____

_____

_____

_____

_____

_____

_____

_____

_____

_____

_____

_____

_____

_____

_____

_____

_____

_____

_____

_____

_____

_____

_____

_____

_____

_____

_____

_____

#4 Flash Tales
(reprehensible, malevolent, chip, delicacy, unforgiving)

The Earthquake
(Neal)

When Cyril first came to live with them, he knew he was in the <u>chips</u>. The Peabodys were putty in his hands. They treated him like royalty, and everything went according to plan until the day the earth moved. The tinkling chandelier swayed above his head and crashed heavily to the floor, narrowly missing him.

Cyril found this <u>reprehensible</u> behavior, and he was <u>unforgiving</u>. The Peabodys tried everything to regain his favor, even offering <u>delicacies</u>, but he turned a <u>malevolent</u> eye on their groveling. They had violated his pride, and after all, cats have their standards.

The Shadow Master
(Sagan)

Thoren stood over the peasants, arms crossed over his chest, eyes cold as ice. The peasants bowed with their foreheads touching the stone-<u>chip</u>-covered ground. Many met their deaths at his <u>malevolent</u> hands. No one knew when his marauders would next attack and loot the village, enslaving the women and children and leaving the men dead in the dirt.

The unforgiving Thoren seemed to appear from the shadows of a reprehensible parallel universe. Each time the survivors recovered and rebuilt, the shadowy hoard infiltrated the village and took their spoils without delicacy. The peasants' only choice — submit or perish.

Chip
(Raker)

Marita glimpsed him through the crowd. What he'd done was reprehensible! Beyond the buffet tables, back under the tents, he mingled with the workers. There! His malevolent eyes caught hers, then slid away.

Other potential victims took hors d'oeuvres, unaware. As he approached the table with another tray of smoked oysters on toast points, Marita stepped back among the partygoers, her unforgiving stare riveting him. She knew the potential harm of each proffered delicacy.

Should she warn the others of his cruel plot, concealing that tiny pearl, resulting in the horrendous chip in her perfect tooth?

Lewis's Strategy
(Sikes)

When Lewis awoke, he craved one of Margo's delicacies. Hearing noises in the kitchen, but smelling nothing, he concluded supper would be a while. Reprehensible as he knew it was, Lewis put his malevolent plan into motion. He leaped onto the counter and glared at

Margo.

"Bad cat. No treat this time."

Surprised at Margo's <u>unforgiving</u> attitude, Lewis crouched and looked away.

Then he saw the <u>chips</u>, crisp and inviting. He pounced. The open bag and Lewis slid off the counter and onto the floor.

In spite of Margo's obvious disapproval, Lewis felt his plan had succeeded.

The Delicacy
(Gendusa-Yokum)

Have you eaten at Captain Kidd's restaurant? Their soft-shell crab Gran Marnier is a <u>delicacy</u> you don't want to miss.

The restaurant is named for a <u>reprehensible</u> old fellow who frequented these shores in the early 1800s. They say folks would quiver at the thought of his bestowing his <u>malevolent</u> presence upon them. His saving grace was that he gave pieces of eight to anyone who prepared an intriguing new version of his favorite soft-shell crab Gran Marnier.

Captain Kidd's last meal was laced with rat poison by an <u>unforgiving</u> soul with a <u>chip</u> on his shoulder.

Now You Try!
(reprehensible, malevolent, chip, delicacy, unforgiving)

_____

_____

_____

_____

_____

_____

_____

_____

_____

_____

_____

_____

_____

_____

_____

_____

_____

_____

_____

_____

_____

_____

_____

_____

#5 Flash Tales
(recipe, humble, providence, mop, basin)

Are You Listening?
(Neal)

"Another church meeting," Ralph muttered to himself as he worked. "I wonder if there really is a God who answers prayers? God, if you're there, Nellie, our boys, and I are barely getting by. I'd sure appreciate some help."

"<u>Providence</u> looks after the <u>humble</u>," intoned the Reverend James as he addressed the finance committee. A clatter sounded in the background as a <u>mop</u> handle struck against the side of a <u>basin</u>.

The clergyman interrupted himself, "That reminds me, Ralph, the janitor, is due for a raise in salary."

He resumed, "But pride is the <u>recipe</u> for disaster."

The Dream
(Sagan)

Emigrating from the old country, Luigi brought the old family <u>recipe</u> with him. The family made it to the Promised Land and found no boundaries to their dreams, save one. Luigi's neighborhood restaurant lasted only until the Depression hit, and his dreams crashed with the stock market.

<u>Mopping</u> his brow, Luigi wondered why <u>Providence</u> robbed him of his dream. For now, he must work at a

humble dishwashing job over a steaming <u>basin</u>. As he toils, he plans and thinks of his nest egg in the mattress. Luigi's dream can begin again with a cart at 11th and Hudson.

Walking?
(Raker)

"Didn't own a car till I was forty." Étienne gestured toward his Mercedes. "<u>Humble</u> beginnings led to a penthouse. Care to come up, ma *chérie*?"

Marie studied him.

"Now I'm head chef at the state capitol. My <u>recipe</u> for jambalaya brought me from Lafayette to <u>Providence</u>. A <u>basin</u> of iced shrimp opened doors."

Marie looked impressed.

"But," he continued, "I've always wanted to live where my ancestors did in Nova Scotia."

Étienne helped Marie into the front seat. "I began by walking to a job <u>mopping</u> floors at Red Lobster. Now I'm 'wokking' my way up the East Coast."

Whatever It Takes
(Sikes)

Millie threw the <u>mop</u> into the closet, grasped the bucket, and struggled upstairs. Water sloshed out as she mounted the steps, but she paid no mind. Her sister Adelle always sidestepped these <u>humble</u> jobs and got the fun ones—like cooking and even using her own <u>recipe</u>.

If <u>Providence</u> wills it, Millie thought, I'll get my revenge.

She planned while filling the <u>basins,</u> then started downstairs. Forgetting about the spilled water, she slipped, then slid down the staircase.

Millie smiled through her pain as her sister cleaned up the mess. That hadn't been the plan, but whatever it takes.

Cold Water
Gendusa-Yokum

LillyBeth was a <u>humble</u> child entrusting her life to <u>Providence</u>. As she struggled to <u>mop</u> the kitchen floor, she dreamed up a cherry-pecan pie <u>recipe</u> to take to the County Fair.

Swishing the heavy, wet mop from side to side, she hurried before her stepmother ordered all hot water turned off for the evening. LillyBeth hated washing her hands in freezing cold water.

She quickly rinsed the mop and bucket. Just then her stepmother stormed in and backhanded LillyBeth to the floor. A nearby <u>basin</u> of water spilled, whereupon the woman slipped and cracked her skull on the brick fireplace.

Now You Try!
(reprehensible, malevolent, chip, delicacy, unforgiving)

_____

_____

_____

_____

_____

_____

_____

_____

_____

_____

_____

_____

_____

_____

_____

_____

_____

_____

_____

_____

_____

_____

#6 Flash Tales
(ingenuous, pernicious, cataclysm, modulate, stockings)

The Deception
(Neal)

Her hand trembled as she hung the Christmas stockings. She was giving a party that evening and should have been in a festive mood, but she couldn't modulate the cataclysm of emotions that swept over her. Ralph sat in a sad, hunched heap; his eyes wells of sorrow.

"Pernicious vermin," she said. "I was so trusting, so ingenuous. I believed everything he told me. 'Ralph's housebroken, honey. Just keep him for me this weekend.'"

Now her stained $125 satin evening shoes sat out in the garage.

"Housebroken, my foot," she said.

The End
(Sagan)

An ingenuous programmer sat in a cold bunker deep in a mountain somewhere in Colorado every night and tugged at her wool stockings. Computer screens provided the only light. Twenty people hunched over their keyboards watching as a pernicious asteroid rolled through space, looming ever larger with each passing day. When would it hit? No one knew.

Scientists and astrophysicists worked increasing hours to find a way to <u>modulate</u> the asteroid's path before a <u>cataclysm</u> ended life on earth. Could they find the answer in time?

The red phone rang. The computer screens went blank. Doomsday arrived too soon.

Vivian
(Raker)

Although <u>ingenuous</u>, Vivian often overreacted. One day—the year she took the vocabulary class—when Orville came home, she wasn't in the house. Then he heard her, screaming from the cliff above, yelling something about a <u>pernicious</u> <u>cataclysm</u>. Terrified, he ran up the trail to rescue her.

At the top Orville folded her in his arms, then begged her to <u>modulate</u> her voice so he could understand what she was trying to tell him. Vivian collapsed against his chest, sobbing.

"What's wrong, my dearest?"

"My stock . . . run, my <u>stocking</u> has a runner!"

Red Is in, Baby
(Sikes)

Doris, although <u>ingenuous</u>, managed to <u>modulate</u> her life, keeping the highs and lows at bay. She knew that to live any other way would be <u>cataclysmic</u>.

A gift of red <u>stockings</u> changed everything. As she marveled at the lovely the red stockings on her delicate feet and slender legs, she realized that those neutral colors, like <u>pernicious</u> beasts, had been eating away at her soul and killing her imagination. No more beiges and grays. Only brights from now on.

Doris grabbed her purse and headed for Wal-Mart.

Righteous Indignation
(Gendusa-Yokum)

His <u>pernicious</u> personality was evident in his venomous insults, yet his understanding wife, Larissa, continued to <u>modulate</u> the family atmosphere, attempting to hold the marriage together. Finally she had to admit the impending <u>cataclysm</u>, especially upon their children.

Since he had no respect for her or their offspring, there was nothing to lose. She decided to approach this self-centered creep in her most <u>ingenuous</u> manner. "You're welcome to leave anytime you want."

He was shocked speechless.

Larissa pulled on her <u>stockings</u>, grabbed her purse, and slammed the door behind her.

He was still there when she got home at 5:00.

Now You Try!
(ingenuous, pernicious, cataclysm, modulate, stockings)

_____

_____

_____

_____

_____

_____

_____

_____

_____

_____

_____

_____

_____

_____

_____

_____

_____

_____

_____

_____

_____

_____

_____

_____

#7 Flash Tales
(ambassador, pennant, fabric, wither, frenzy)

The Lesson
(Neal)

The <u>ambassador</u>'s daughter Jeannine was playing church. She was reading the book of Ruth from the Bible to <u>Frenzy</u>, the bloodhound who lay dozing by the fire. Jeannine's mother, Laura, came into the room wearing an evening dress of bright <u>pennant</u>-red <u>fabric</u>. Lacking only her evening gloves to be ready for the reception, she paused to listen to her daughter.

"Now, <u>Frenzy</u>, pay attention to the lesson. Ruth said, '<u>Wither</u> thou goest, I will go.'"

"No, dear." Laura laughed. "She said, 'Whither thou goest.'"

"Whither, wither," said the little girl with a frown. "I thought she was talking to Naomi."

Independence
(Sagan)

Women in Victorian dresses and large hats baked in the African sun. Men suffered in wool <u>fabric</u> suits.

"We shall <u>wither</u> away to nothing before he arrives," a large woman proclaimed.

"Why such a <u>frenzy</u> over his coming?" asked another woman.

"Too long we've waited for home rule," a young man snorted.

"He is a representative of the Crown," said a tall man behind them.

After what seemed like hours, a <u>pennant</u> appeared through the heat waves. Soldiers marched two abreast escorting the <u>ambassador</u> to the colonial governor's palace. After hours of negotiations, Britain granted independence to the colony.

The Ambassador
Raker

The <u>ambassador</u> lounged in his limo. A pennant of bright <u>fabric</u> <u>frenzied</u> by speed-caused wind stood erect on the fender.

"Quick, to the embassy. I'm meeting Ursula at the portico. She'll be packed for the weekend at the Cape."

The iron gate opened at their approach. Ursula was indeed ready. She rushed out, carrying her small valise, but brushed past the limo, through the gate, and toward a crimson Jaguar parked at the curb. A robust fellow held the door and helped her in, her bag in back. They roared away.

The ambassador noticed his <u>pennant</u> had <u>withered</u>.

The Ortiz File
(Sikes)

Natalie Ortiz paused in front of the brick and stone building and nodded to her companion. "I'll be along in a minute."

She reached into her pocket and stroked the <u>pennant</u>, the tattered <u>fabric</u> all she had left of her father. Exiled from the country he loved, she'd watched in anguish as he <u>withered</u> away. After his death, her anger evolved into courage. Her life became a <u>frenzy</u> of activity, focused solely on her goal—retribution.

Taking a deep breath, she strode toward the entrance. A uniformed man opened the door and bowed. "Welcome, <u>Ambassador</u> Ortiz."

Hot Water
Gendusa-Yokum

The foreign <u>ambassador</u> raged in a fanatical <u>frenzy</u>. His newly hired tailor had smushed his wool tailcoat by cleaning it with such hot water that the <u>fabric</u> shrank and <u>withered</u>.

Now his coattails resembled stringy <u>pennants</u>, unduly accentuating his oversized derriere. He demanded the tailor provide him with a new suit, but the tailor was under contract to his employer, who refused to be held responsible, especially since the tailor was on loan from an overseas outfit. The best they suggested would be to steam press the suit and try to stretch it to its original shape.

No guarantees.

Now You Try!
(ambassador, pennant, fabric, wither, frenzy)

#8 Flash Tales
(barren, masterful, pique, gardenia, malarkey)

The Gesture
(Neal)

Valerie sniffed the gardenia corsage. What a heavenly scent, she thought. It carries you right away. She frowned as she remembered the argument of the night before. Who else but Lionel would have tried to put a <u>masterful</u> spin on an explosion that was no more than a fit of <u>pique</u>—utterly <u>barren</u> of either reason or logic? It was exceeded only by the excuses he came up with today that were supposed to pass for an apology. <u>Malarkey</u>.

Still, the <u>gardenia</u> was a nice touch.

She closed her eyes and smiled as she breathed in the intoxicating fragrance.

Reverie From Chaos
(Sagan)

John <u>Malarkey</u> gazed across the North African <u>barren</u> desert. He wondered how long they would wait for Rommel's tanks to attack again. Yesterday, the British and American troops had outflanked the Desert Fox with a <u>masterful</u> stroke of genius by General Patton.

Behind a rocky embankment, John took a sip of lukewarm water and felt <u>piqued</u> over their conditions, short rations, and water. They hadn't changed clothes in days.

They endured hours of thundering cannon.

Then, John thought about Lucy. He'd given her gardenias and a ring. He dreamt of his return home and marrying Lucy when the war ended.

Centerpiece
(Raker)

Edgar had a masterful plan—delivery van up the back road, away from the house, barren-looking pasture land for the setting.

Gardenias were arranged in a starburst. Edgar stripped. Cell phone in hand, he stepped to the center of the display and reclined, face up. He punched in her number.

"Rosamond, . . ."

"Edgar, I'm piqued at you."

"No, darling, don't just peek. Come out here and take a look."

"Sweetie, this is not the time for such malarkey. My bridge club is here, out on the terrace. They're using binoculars to admire your gardenias."

The Gardenia Episode
(Sikes)

"Why are you so piqued?" Myrtle asked as she bent over and gently ran her fingers through her niece's hair.

Five-year-old Lucy stomped her feet and tried to sound

masterful. "I want that gardenia."

Myrtle straightened to her full height. "But it's the only bloom. Without flowers, my garden will look barren."

"But this one will make Spot smell better, Aunt Myrtle. Then he can come in the house and play with me."

"That's a lot of malarkey," Myrtle said.

Lucy crossed her arms over her chest and said, "Please?"

Myrtle relented. "Oh, go ahead."

Prize Gardenias
Gendusa-Yokum

"Quincy, I'm upset. Newton's Landscape said the area where I grow my prize gardenias must be barren of all plants for six months. I won't be able to enter the Prize-Winning Gardenias $1,000.00 Contest."

"I understand your pique, Henrietta, but six months is malarkey. With your masterful touch, we can prepare the soil with organic fertilizers and have your gardenias blooming in no time."

"Thanks. I put down soil sterilizer to clean things up."

"Now you can't grow anything! You'll have to replace all the soil!"

"Let's do it. The Garden Homes contest finalizes in June. I've got to win."

Now You Try!

(barren, masterful, pique, gardenia, malarkey)

_____

_____

_____

_____

_____

_____

_____

_____

_____

_____

_____

_____

_____

_____

_____

_____

_____

_____

_____

_____

_____

_____

_____

_____

#9 Flash Tales
(omit, star, irascible, bricks, rectitude)

Wicked Kitty
(Neal)

The Cliffords were completely under the thumb of their black cat, Catullus. Wherever he sat became a throne, but his favorite place was the living room. He entered with the panache of a silent-screen <u>star</u>, sweeping his bushy tail across the floor behind him like an emperor's cloak. He took his position on the <u>brick</u> hearth and turned his <u>irascible</u> countenance toward his family. With what <u>rectitude</u> he meted out judgments! No service he required could be <u>omitted</u>, or his wrath would be forthcoming.

The poor Cliffords had wanted a pet, but now were mere dust under his chariot wheels.

Discovery
(Sagan)

Phineas became more <u>irascible</u> by the year. Dathan, his assistant, loved studying the night skies. He always carried the telescope to the top a nearby hill. Phineas studied angles, adjusted the lenses and tripod legs until he got it right.

Dathan sat on some ancient <u>bricks</u> and wrote down what his master said. He weathered Phineas's moods and tantrums for a peek through the telescope. Finally, Dathan no longer enjoyed gazing at the stars, sharing discoveries.

His master <u>omitted</u> him from any recognition. Dathan found no <u>rectitude</u>, only scorn, but in his heart he remembered the <u>star</u>—his star.

In Austin
(Raker)

A crowd gathered outside the club to pay tribute to a musician. Public officials would decide. One nominee under consideration was controversial.

"He's too <u>irascible</u>," said the feisty governor.

"No <u>rectitude</u>," retorted a conservative senator, thrice married.

The owner of the establishment rose. "<u>Omit</u> character as criteria." He marched out, removed <u>bricks</u> from the sidewalk, replacing them with a <u>star</u>. His decision made prior to the discussion, he'd ordered the inscription naming his favorite performer.

Hubbub announced arrival of that scruffy celebrity on a matching Harley. The rider was singing, "On the road again."

Star's Opus
(Sikes)

Tap-tap, tap-tap. <u>Star</u> didn't worry about her hunt-and-peck system. Her fingers always found the right keys. Why be concerned about <u>rectitude</u>? The burning within her to write her story, <u>brick</u> by brick, and to <u>omit</u> nothing left her no time to learn keyboarding.

Her siblings and friends teased her, telling her that she wasn't capable of such a feat considering her <u>irascible</u> behavior.

"Phooey," she'd say and continue on.

One day Star overheard her mother say to her father, "You know, she's really determined about this project. She just might be published by her sixth birthday."

Star Crossed
(Gendusa-Yokum)

That <u>irascible</u> choleric, an extreme personification of <u>rectitude</u>, <u>omits</u> consideration for everyone but himself, hurling verbal <u>bricks</u> at anyone who crosses this brilliant self-centered <u>star</u>. His day of justification came when he was caught in one of his own schemes to attempt self-righteous circumvention of the law.

And when he needed the moral support of others, no one would step to his side, for he had spent all his "quality-points" of friendship ruining the lives of many colleagues and conscientious citizens.

In his climb to the top over the devastated carcasses of others, he now stood despised and alone.

Now You Try!
(omit, star, irascible, bricks, rectitude)

_____
_____
_____
_____
_____
_____
_____
_____
_____
_____
_____
_____
_____
_____
_____
_____
_____
_____
_____
_____
_____
_____
_____

#10 Flash Tales
(education, deliberate, bumptious, literature, fragile)

Educated Aesthetes
(Neal)

Everard and his friend Boris could be <u>bumptious</u> in their literary opinions. They met in a bistro called The Raised Eyebrow to <u>deliberate</u>.

"*Ulysses* is a brilliant work," said Everard, "but impenetrable for most readers."

"I agree," said Boris. "Definitely not for the masses."

"However, anyone can read Hemingway, but he seems to me to have a <u>fragile</u> and tenuous connection to what we call <u>literature</u>."

"Just so. He would never be published today."

"Do you recall the jest? How would Hemingway answer the question, 'Why did the chicken cross the road?'"

"To die."

"Alone."

"In the rain."

Triumphant
(Sagan)

The <u>fragile</u> youth stood with knees knocking, hoping her classmates wouldn't snicker. A <u>bumptious</u> boy, who taunted her daily, grinned from his seat. Laurel began her recitation. She cleared her throat and made a false start.

Again, Laurel began reciting from her chosen literature. This time her voice rang clear and deliberate. She focused her eyes on a painting of her own mother hanging on the back wall. As the first woman with an education as a full professor at the school, she provided inspiration for Laurel. The young girl took heart, overcame her fears, and received her first standing ovation.

Beloved Son
(Raker)

Reginald met Eleanor in Victorian literature class. They married and led deliberate lives—studying, collecting, researching, writing. Living frugally, they saved for their son's education before he was even conceived.

They treated little Rockwell as if made of fragile crystal, with Bach and Beethoven in his nursery. But by two, Rocky was a bumptious lad. His parents lamented his trading—at twelve—his violin for a guitar, playing Led Zeppelin. They grieved when he left Harvard for a punk band.

But they forgave their wayward son when his first gold album provided their retirement in the south of France.

Love at First Flight
(Sikes)

Susan received quite an <u>education</u> during her flight, although she didn't <u>deliberately</u> set out to. A handsome man sat beside her, and they spoke of <u>literature</u>, religion, science, and politics. Susan marveled at the compatibility between them. When he asked if he could see her later, she eagerly said yes and wondered if she'd finally met Mister Right.

When he retrieved their bags, her breath caught in her throat as she watched his muscles ripple beneath his shirt.

Dreams are <u>fragile</u>.

After they disembarked, a gorgeous woman ran into Mr. Right's arms.

Susan sighed. "Wouldn't you know, another Mr. <u>Bumptious</u>."

To Each His Own
(Gendusa-Yokum)

From the time of birth, twins may demonstrate opposite temperaments. Whereas one may be <u>bumptious</u> and carefree, his brother may be introspective and <u>deliberate</u>. Family dynamics and even body type contribute to the development of confidence and personality.

Crises often arise when neighborhood playground athletics become too one-sided. The macho fellows are best liked and always chosen when sides team up.

This happened to a <u>fragile</u> youth, Frankie, who felt left out and close to tears. Suddenly a brainstorm resolved his dilemma. Wielding pad and pencil, he appointed himself scorekeeper. Everyone cheered.

Research <u>literature</u> in <u>educational</u> psychology calls this "compensation."

Now You Try!
(education, deliberate, bumptious, literature, fragile)

_____

_____

_____

_____

_____

_____

_____

_____

_____

_____

_____

_____

_____

_____

_____

_____

_____

_____

_____

_____

_____

_____

_____

#11 Flash Tales
(hypnotic, chartreuse, accent, lock, flower)

War Is Hell
(Neal)

I am in the <u>flower</u> of my manhood, Cedric thought as he sipped the glass of <u>Chartreuse</u>. I have a <u>hypnotic</u> power over these American women. It is partly my English <u>accent</u>, of course. It fits my purposes like a key in a <u>lock</u>. My experiences in the war have given me a mystique, a hint of the dangerous, alert animal. He luxuriated in his power.

His wife, Elizabeth, observed him sadly. It is such a pity, she thought. The Great War was over thirty years ago, yet he has never really come back home again.

Forbidden
(Sagan)

The ragged boy stood outside the estate's imposing walls and filigreed gate. Peter peered through the gate and ran his fingers over the ornate <u>lock</u>. His thoughts wandered to when this forbidden scene had been his home.

Once Peter picked a <u>chartreuse</u> <u>flower</u> for his adoring mother. She smiled and ruffled his hair, then said in her Irish <u>accent</u>, "Thank ya, luv." But, his gentle mother, Sarah, died last winter after a carriage accident killed his father.

After Peter's uncle inherited the estate, everything changed. Now Peter shivered outside, listening to <u>hypnotic</u> strains of music drift over the wall.

Hypnotic
(Raker)

A shadow crossed Gertrude's window. Moonlight silhouetted a virile form. Gertrude ducked beneath the sill. Moving the curtain slightly, she peeked out. The figure strode onto the porch. Gertrude raced to the door and checked the latch.

A fist pounded on the wood under the pane. Gertrude glimpsed, in the porch light's glow, his chapeau, bearing—instead of a feather—a <u>chartreuse</u> <u>flower</u>.

Intriguing.

"Let me in," an <u>accented</u> voice demanded.

"Who is it?"

"Stanislaus."

Stanislaus? Gertrude didn't know any Stanislaus. The flower, the voice, the name—all had their <u>hypnotic</u> effect. She <u>unlocked</u> the door.

The Stones Hold the Answer
(Sikes)

Janet rattled the doorknob again, but the <u>lock</u> held. She turned to Bill and asked, "Where is Penelope?"

"Let's try the back," he whispered.

His calm manner didn't have its usual <u>hypnotic</u> effect, and she shivered.

Janet followed Bill along the path through the <u>flower</u> bed. "Penelope will have a heart attack when she sees us."

Bill stopped short. "I don't think so."

"Why?" Janet asked. She peered around him, then screamed.

Splotches of dark red <u>accented</u> the <u>chartreuse</u> cushions on the lawn swing. Beside it, as cold as the stones beneath her, lay Penelope.

Lost in Time
(Gendusa-Yokum)

The <u>chartreuse</u> <u>flowers</u> with purple and green <u>accents</u> on Zach's couch seemed to have a <u>hypnotic</u> effect. He'd get so relaxed he'd fall asleep.

He promised himself this time he must stay awake. Chemistry finals were tomorrow. "I could fix a pot of black coffee, but if I drink that, I'll be awake all night and feel groggy in the morning," he cautioned himself.

Suddenly, he had a brainstorm. "I know. I'll go to bed, set my alarm for 3 a.m., get up and start studying. With my review fresh in mind, I know I can <u>lock</u> in that A!"

Now You Try!
(hypnotic, chartreuse, accent, lock, flower)

_____

_____

_____

_____

_____

_____

_____

_____

_____

_____

_____

_____

_____

_____

_____

_____

_____

_____

_____

_____

_____

_____

_____

_____

#12 Flash Tales
(deck, chicanery, rapier, cricket, button)

History Records
(Neal)

Sir Winston's waistcoat <u>buttons</u> underwent a strain as he sat on the <u>deck</u> expounding in vivid language on Hitler's behavior. His <u>rapier</u> wit had entertained President Roosevelt all during their conversation, but now Sir Winston came to the point.

He stabbed the air with his cigar as he spoke. "It's just not <u>cricket</u>! This last sortie is insufferable! It's <u>chicanery</u> of the highest order," he bellowed. "With the help of our allies, we'll grind this miserable paperhanger's bones into a fine powder and his goose-stepping henchmen along with him!"

Actually, history records that he chose more colorful words.

The Quest
(Sagan)

The firelight flickered in the trees. Shadows danced across the night. The hooded figure slumped against his bundle listening to a persistent <u>cricket</u>. Half under a blanket, but well within reach, lay a <u>rapier's</u> exposed ornate hilt.

Nevil's eyes searched the darkness. Would the stranger come? Would he join the quest?

Nevil fastened the <u>buttons</u> on his vest against the cold and remembered his companions' <u>chicanery</u> and frivolity on the ship's <u>deck</u> their last night together.

Then, in the mists of dawn, the stranger appeared. Nevil no longer searched alone.

Rupert
(Raker)

"Dar-ling," whined Madeline, zipping the wedding dress, "why Rupert? With those silver <u>buttons</u>, that pretentious <u>rapier</u>, his ridiculous <u>chicanery</u>?"

"Mummy, you know I love him."

"Yes, dear, but you could have loved strong young Jack, the former college quarterback and newly promoted law partner."

"But, Mummy . . ."

"Or perhaps Captain Malcolm. You could have lounged on the <u>deck</u> of his yacht and lived in the islands."

"Jiminy cricket, Mummy, you know why. Remember my bedtime doll?"

"Yes?"

"It was never my bubby's G.I. Joe nor his Troy Aikman figure. It was always my soft, fuzzy Nutcracker doll."

The Duke of Norfolk
(Sikes)

Humphrey gestured toward the portrait. "Miles, I present my great-great-great grandfather, the Duke of Norfolk."

"Bloody impressive, Lord Griffith."

"He was a distinguished military commander."

"Obviously. He looks ready to draw his rapier."

"It is rumored many heads were separated from their bodies with that."

"Not very cricket, I'd say."

Humphrey chuckled. "True, but I've been told anyone who stood in his way was soon decked. See the buttons on his jacket and the pocket watch and chain? All gold."

"Really now. Where are they?"

"Some chicanery went on among his children, and they disappeared."

"Ah, chips off the old block."

Winter Wishes
Gendusa-Yokum

Miss Squirrel scampered across the deck of the porch. "Mr. Cricket, I was saving some wool to place in my nest before winter sets in. I wish I could find it. Do you recall seeing my bit of fabric anywhere?"

Chewing on string attached to a brown button, Cranston Cricket chirped, "If wishes were fishes, your brain would be swimming, Miss Squirrel."

His <u>chicanery</u> and sharp tone cut into Miss Squirrel's sensibilities like a <u>rapier</u>. "Such a thieving little twerp, that cranky ol' cricket," she thought. "See if I give him any crumbles from the acorns I hid yesterday."

Now You Try!
(deck, chicanery, rapier, cricket, button)

_____

_____

_____

_____

_____

_____

_____

_____

_____

_____

_____

_____

_____

_____

_____

_____

_____

_____

_____

_____

_____

_____

_____

_____

_____

#13 Flash Tales
(nebbish, grapes, cup, minimal, chortle, sunset)

Va-Va-Voom!
(Neal)

Lucy <u>chortled</u> to herself and nibbled on some <u>grapes</u> as she drove toward the <u>sunset</u>. She recalled her triumphal entry into the workplace this morning. She had been trying to attract the attention of David, her handsome coworker, but he rarely looked up when she walked past his desk. Until today, she had been regarded as a <u>nebbish</u>, of such <u>minimal</u> worth as to be invisible. All that changed this morning because she had slipped breast enhancers inside her bra, increasing her <u>cup</u> size from an A to a C. Voila! Suddenly, she was visible.

The Prize
(Sagan)

Competing gourmet chefs developed new dishes and lavish presentations for months in advance. Finally, they descended on the California wine country for the challenge.

David <u>chortled</u> as he watched the <u>sunset</u> on the last day of competition. "Todd is such a <u>nebbish</u>," he thought. Todd's idea of a presentation consisted of over-sized platters with <u>minimal</u> delicacies. The two men competed for the crystal trophy every year.

Finally, the microphone crackled, and the room grew silent. David smirked and stepped forward. Then, a clear voice announced, "Todd's <u>grape</u> <u>cups</u> formed the *pièce de résistance* and stole the show."

David's jaw dropped.

The Nebbish
(Raker)

Marvin was a <u>nebbish</u>. He always had been, kind of a <u>minimal</u> guy. Nobody remembered him from class. Coworkers didn't notice if he stayed home sick. He frequently got cut off in traffic.

Inside his apartment, however, he was different—clever, fit, glistening in a way. But that was when he was alone.

At the company picnic that year, however, Marvin took a <u>cup</u> of the <u>grape</u> and then another. He sat in the glow of the <u>sunset</u>, watching the ladies' softball team, and began to <u>chortle</u> to himself. He knew what they didn't.

And they still don't.

What Happened to George?
(Sikes)

George raised his cup to the <u>sunset</u>, a <u>minimal</u> tribute considering what this day had brought. It was a bit <u>nebbish</u>, though, since this was the sixth <u>cup</u> he'd raised. Through bleary eyes, he watched Susanne walking beneath the <u>grape</u> arbor.

"Shushanne!" George shouted.

"Look at you," Susanne said. "You're a disgrace and

don't deserve the millions Uncle Vic left you."

"Dish-graish? Me?" George chortled and took a few steps backward.

"You'd better watch it, George. There's a cliff behind you."

"I know where I'm going. Uncle Vic took care of that." George stumbled and disappeared.

Tales in Red Sunset
(Gendusa-Yokum)

The rosy illumination of the sunset filtered through the windows, drawing Meg outside into the cool dusk. Warmed by her cup of hot raspberry tea, she rocked contentedly in the swing on the vine-latticed veranda.

Suddenly a chortle — so minimal, so nebbishy — startled Meg from her reverie. What could that be? Remaining very still, she scanned the surroundings for its source. A beautiful, red-breasted robin just five feet away struggled to disengage from a twisted grapevine.

Using a thin stick, with the slightest movement possible, she lifted the offending branch, and the small creature hopped away to safety.

Now You Try!

(nebbish, grapes, cup, minimal, chortle, sunset)

_____

_____

_____

_____

_____

_____

_____

_____

_____

_____

_____

_____

_____

_____

_____

_____

_____

_____

_____

_____

_____

_____

_____

#14 Flash Tales
(abbreviated, screamed, mud, vaporize, daughter)

Hissy
(Neal)

Little Alice sat daydreaming about <u>mud</u> pies in the living room where Big Mother was deep in conversation with her <u>daughter</u> Lillian Blanche. The daydream <u>vaporized</u> just as Big Mother came to the <u>abbreviated</u> end of her story.

"And he talked on for so long," Big Mother said, "I thought I was going to jump up and go to <u>screaming</u>."

Alice grinned. She tried to picture Big Mother with her dignified, grandmotherly presence suddenly leaping to her feet in the midst of a crowd, screaming and pulling her hair. No, it would never happen.

Shelter from the Storm
(Sagan)

Wanda and her <u>daughter</u> slogged through the <u>mud</u> and heavy rain looking for shelter. They'd pulled themselves from the wreckage. The injured girl grew weaker by the mile. Finally, they saw distant cabin lights. Relief swept over Wanda. Now, help was at hand.

She pounded on the cabin door and <u>screamed</u> for help. The hinges creaked, and lantern light spilled out onto the porch. Someone pulled them inside. Wanda gave an

<u>abbreviated</u> version of their mishap while the woman attended to their care. She applied a <u>mud</u> poultice to the daughter's shoulder and <u>vaporized</u> herbs for congestion. Safe at last!

Dark Pool
(Raker)

Zobar knew the outside atmosphere was safe, but he worried. He watched through the wall of the Lexan dome as his <u>daughter</u> explored the edge of the swamp. Finally he went into his virtual exerciser.

Zobar heard his communicator's <u>abbreviated</u> beep, and he switched on. Nirian <u>screamed</u>. He ran through the air lock. Her head protruded above the dark muck—terror in her eyes, a gooey substance almost to her nose.

Tears streamed down his cheeks. "Sweetheart, I'll take care of you!"

Zobar raised his blaster, pulled the trigger.

Nirian stood in a dry basin.

Success. He'd <u>vaporized</u> the <u>mud</u>.

A State of Undress
(Sikes)

Amber pranced by in her <u>abbreviated</u> skirt. Jane grimaced. It was as if all arguments she'd given Jim about his <u>daughter's</u> modesty, or lack of it, had <u>vaporized</u>.

She formed a plan. Donning her work gloves, she

uncoiled the garden hose, turned on the water, and trained the stream toward the alley until <u>muddy</u> lakes appeared.

Back in the house, she called, "Amber, take out the trash, please."

Amber protested, but obeyed.

When Jane heard Amber's <u>scream</u>, she chuckled, then muttered, "Poor thing. She must be a mess."

Mud Puddles
(Gendusa-Yokum)

"Rosie, let's keep Poochie inside. It's raining, and we don't want him to get <u>muddy</u> feet on our carpet."

Rosie and Poochie watched from their patio door.

Just as Marcella answered an important phone call, she heard Rosie <u>screaming</u>. She dropped the receiver and ran. Rosie was lying in a puddle outside in the freezing wind and rain. Marcella scooped her up. Rosie and Poochie were wet, muddy, and shivering.

Rosie sniffled. "Poochie jumped out."

That evening Marcella ran the <u>vaporizer</u> to ease Rosie's head cold and cough.

They had an <u>abbreviated</u> holiday that weekend, nursing that sick little <u>daughter</u>.

Now You Try!
(abbreviated, screamed, mud, vaporize, daughter)

_____

_____

_____

_____

_____

_____

_____

_____

_____

_____

_____

_____

_____

_____

_____

_____

_____

_____

_____

_____

_____

_____

_____

_____

#15 Flash Tales
(critical, cap, changeling, confused, generous)

Perspective
(Neal)

The fastidiously dressed Evelyn turned a <u>critical</u> eye on her teenaged daughter Priscilla. Despite a <u>generous</u> clothing allowance, she wore only jeans, T-shirts, and baseball <u>caps</u>. Surely this child was <u>confused</u> at birth, she thought, a <u>changeling</u>.

She heard her own mother's voice in her head, "Evelyn, do stand up straight. You look just like a question mark. I can't imagine how any child of mine could care so little about her appearance."

Evelyn smiled at her daughter and said, "I wish my mother could have lived to see what a lovely young girl you have grown up to be."

Missing
(Sagan)

Jenny shivered in spite of the wool blanket over her lap. Radiator heat waves rose across the window as she watched large snowflakes falling from an ever-darkening sky. Authorities continued searching for her missing child. They'd acted <u>critical</u> of her failings and were confused at her description of him.

Mrs. Abrams, her <u>generous</u> neighbor, waited with her.

Jenny hoped her <u>changeling</u> child would look like a human when they found him.

Just before dark, detectives arrived holding a quilt bundled around a small figure. Jenny recognized the <u>cap</u>. She ran to embrace her child.

Virgil
(Raker)

"I'm <u>confused</u>."

"Me too."

"Virgil is wearing his <u>cap</u> on backwards."

"And he's <u>generous</u>. He offered to loan me his truck."

"Wow. That's not like Virgil."

"And he complimented Katherine."

"Really? He's usually so <u>critical</u>."

"I know."

"So, what do you think?"

"It's obvious. He's a changeling."

"He can't be. A changeling is a child secretly substituted by fairies for the parents' real child in infancy. And Virgil's definitely NOT a baby."

"Okay. So, an old duckling is called a duck?"

"Yep."

"Virgil is an old changeling, so let's call him a 'change' — one grownup swapped for another."

The Rebellious One
(Sikes)

Greg shouted, "I'm sick of you." He grabbed his baseball <u>cap</u> and stormed out, ignoring his mother's pleas.

Marian felt a hand on her shoulder.

"What did Greg do this time? I heard the argument all the way from the garage," her husband said.

"I'm so <u>confused</u>, Ray," Marian said. "Maybe we've been too <u>critical</u>, too . . ."

"No. If anything we've been too <u>generous</u>. We've taught him right from wrong. It's time to let go."

"I can't, Ray." Marian sighed. "But do you think we might have been given a <u>changeling</u> seventeen years ago?"

The Precious Gift
(Gendusa-Yokum)

"What a precious baby. Here is a gift from our hospital nurses to newborns."

"How <u>generous</u> and thoughtful. This <u>cap</u> is perfect for chilly weather."

"Here, let me place it on your baby's head. See, the boys get blue ones."

"Thank you. I must hurry now. My mother is waiting."

C8C8C8

"Mom, why do you look so <u>confused</u>?"

61

"Martha, I don't want to be <u>critical</u>, but I don't remember Bobby having a birthmark under his chin."

"Oh, Mom, that woman at the hospital picked up one baby, then another! Are you thinking this is a <u>changeling</u> and not my baby?"

Now You Try!

(critical, cap, changeling, confused, generous)

_____
_____
_____
_____
_____
_____
_____
_____
_____
_____
_____
_____
_____
_____
_____
_____
_____
_____
_____
_____
_____
_____
_____
_____
_____
_____
_____
_____

#16 Flash Tales
(aggregate, conservation, bones, harbor, conducive)

The Committee
(Neal)

"Will the meeting please come to order," shouted the chairman of the Conservation Committee. "We cannot come to agreement if we harbor resentments and continue to pick over the aggregate bones of past differences. It is not conducive to unity and progress. We must take the high road," he said, gesturing with a sweep of his arm, hand upturned.

"Yeah," said a voice from the corner. "Somebody make a motion to adjourn. My dinner's getting cold."

"I so move."

"All those in favor say aye."

"Aye."

"The ayes have it. At last, we are in agreement. The meeting is adjourned."

Preservation
(Sagan)

The conservation committee held an emergency meeting. It must stop developers from swallowing up every available property overlooking the harbor. If not, then their quiet coastal community as they knew it would disappear. Investors found the town conducive to resorts and condos—each with an ocean view.

This morning while excavating for a hotel foundation, the workers found ancient <u>bones</u> in a layer of <u>aggregate</u> not far from the beach. Committee lawyers filed an injunction to stop the building project in favor of creating an archeological dig rather than a resort. The villagers stopped this hotel project, but not others.

Found
(Raker)

Herbert's votes against <u>conservation</u> and social reform led the senator to be labeled conservative. But his clandestine relationship with his beautiful secretary was obviously liberal.

Illicit affairs are not <u>conducive</u> to getting votes. His constituents knew the election was lost. But what were the facts? There were only presumptions.

Until today. Her <u>bones</u> were found on the rugged coast, five miles from the nearest <u>harbor</u>. Did the <u>aggregate</u> evidence point to the legislator from California? The nation waited. But now the public knows. Herbert just turned himself in to the U.S. marshal.

The Gathering
(Sikes)

"Tom, you've labored for <u>conservation</u> all your adult life. Why quit now?" Viola shaded her eyes as she scanned the <u>harbor</u>.

"I don't have it in me anymore, Viola. Another confrontation is not <u>conducive</u> to the survival of these old <u>bones</u>."

"But, Tom, facing this untimely <u>aggregate</u> of fortune seekers could provide you with a living legacy — your one chance to stave off the onslaught and save this seashore for the creatures that live here."

Tom pointed to the approaching gaggle of interlopers.

"Viola, when have sea turtles and least terns ever scared away land developers?"

Lost in Innocence
Gendusa-Yokum

Following a small <u>aggregate</u> path through the woods and along the pristine lake, we wondered what could have happened. The local citizenry acknowledged that the forbidden forest would be <u>conducive</u> to exploration and possible unforeseen dangers by curious teenagers.

With emphasis on <u>conservation</u>, everything past the <u>harbor</u> remained off-limits. The overgrowth of shrubs, trees, and bushes was virtually impassable.

In the thickest underbrush of these dense woods, youthful hikers, playing a game of pirates searching for hidden treasure, stumbled upon tattered pieces of fabric and scattered <u>bones</u>.

A faded blue head scarf and a small, rusty pedometer lay nearby.

Now You Try!
(aggregate, conservation, bones, harbor, conducive)

_____
_____
_____
_____
_____
_____
_____
_____
_____
_____
_____
_____
_____
_____
_____
_____
_____
_____
_____
_____
_____
_____
_____

#17 Flash Tales
(raucous, canyon, stately, granite, electrifying)

Discovery
(Neal)

Raucous parties did not agree with the Dunstables. Mava Dunstable was a stately woman, quiet and dignified. Her husband, Hal, was set in his ways, as granite-faced and changeless as the terrain of a canyon. A scene of epic proportions took place when Hal and Mava returned early from a trip to find their home filled with electrifying music, pizza and beer containers, and the many disheveled friends of their daughter Hermione.

"But you said to mix with our neighbors," accused Hermione.

"We didn't know," rumbled her father, "when we moved to the Hamptons that the neighbors would be Hottentots!"

The Light Show
(Sagan)

Executives and their wives celebrated a record year at the CEO's stately home built on granite cliffs overlooking the canyon. The group laughed and enjoyed each other's company. Their raucous behavior kept them from noticing the rising storm.

An electrifying flash and thunderous sound deafened the guests. Lights went out. Men gasped and women screamed.

Unruffled, the hostess lighted candles while the host poured everyone another glass of champagne. They watched nature's light show through full-length windows. The magnificent display moved across the canyon, breaking up over the far rim. God's entertainment.

Fear
(Raker)

Timmy squatted, pushing the plastic car through his newly created road. Above ponderosa pines soared the grandeur of <u>granite</u> <u>canyon</u> walls. On a lower cliff, a cougar crouched in <u>stately</u> immobility.

From the camper, Cheryl perceived the scene with startling clarity. But all changed with <u>electrifying</u> speed. The <u>raucous</u> call of a raven broke the silence as he swooped, almost within reach of the tawny figure. A paw flicked out, too far. The cat toppled from his perch, landing in the dust as Cheryl yanked Timmy to safety.

The ebony bird soared skyward, muttering, "Nevermore."

Montana's Quake Lake
(Sikes)

For years travelers camped in a beautiful valley at the base of a mountain near the Madison River. But one night the ground shook, and centuries-old rock, stone, and dirt dislodged and crashed down the mountain, sweeping away everything. The debris became a natural dam and a grave for the unfortunate campers.

Today the stately canyon walls rise hundreds of feet from Quake Lake's edge, thrusting their granite ramparts into the clouds, the stillness broken only by the raucous calls of ravens. But this peaceful scene belies the electrifying events of a half century ago, when the mountain fell.

Mountain Majesty
(Gendusa-Yokum)

Driving through the canyons in Colorado gives visitors the impression of being surrounded by gigantic stately castles of impenetrable granite. The massive stone structures change colors from rust to maroon and black to silvery blue. Silence is broken by raucous waterfalls, electrifying bird calls, and intermittent grinding intrusions of motorcycles.

To mountain climbers, the challenges of reaching mountain peaks may be the ultimate high, but their victory can be only bittersweet when someone is left by the wayside to die of thirst.

Stopping to give precious water, the good Samaritan forfeits short-lived glory for everlasting nobility.

Now You Try!
(raucous, canyon, stately, granite, electrifying)

_____

_____

_____

_____

_____

_____

_____

_____

_____

_____

_____

_____

_____

_____

_____

_____

_____

_____

_____

_____

_____

_____

#18 Flash Tales
(slovenly, revolution, myriad, libations, recalcitrant)

And Round She Goes
(Neal)

For handsome young Phillip, life held a <u>myriad</u> of choices. He was intelligent and well-spoken, but had a <u>recalcitrant</u> streak, so he pursued a languid profession. His smartly-dressed form stood out against the <u>slovenly</u> crowd in the casino as he leaned against the roulette table to place a bet. He accepted a <u>libation</u> from the comely waitress and waited for the <u>revolution</u> of the wheel to cease.

"Double zero wins," called the croupier, pushing a sizable pile of chips toward Phillip. He smiled and pocketed his winnings. Phillip usually won. He always bet with the house.

The General
(Sagan)

General George Washington stood with his aide, feeling disheartened at what he saw. This ragtag army would never win the <u>revolution</u> by defeating the well-trained British armies. These would-be soldiers provided a <u>myriad</u> of reasons why Washington contemplated resigning and returning home. <u>Recalcitrant</u> men wandered from shelter to shelter or huddled around small fires. Their slovenly habits included a preference for libations over liberty.

Washington felt depressed until he received Martha's encouraging letter. Maybe the colonies could win independence. With the arrival of General von Steuben, the army took shape before Washington's eyes. He hoped for victory.

Revolution
(Raker)

Bridget had been a recalcitrant child. As a teenager, she'd been slovenly, infuriating her parents. Of course, she'd partaken of myriad opportunities for libation, much more than her share. The community judged her a ne'er-do-well.

But gradually, she'd focused, trained dutifully, and planned. Her talents gradually combined with those who shared her passion.

The crowd rose up behind Bridget, cheering, excited.

Though she had her back to them, she went to a *plié*, then an arabesque, commanding their attention with her fuchsia tutu. And then Bridget spun.

Ultimately the almost-perfect revolution was a resounding success.

Dr. Gottchalk's Success
(Sikes)

Dr. Gottchalk busied himself with myriad tasks in his laboratory. At five o'clock, his wife brought him his daily libation. Although he insisted on a regular schedule, his grooming was <u>slovenly</u>, and friends noticed how <u>recalcitrant</u> he was about his experiments.

For months he'd tried to reduce the number of <u>revolutions</u> per minute it would take for the propeller on his invention to work correctly. It was time for the test. He flipped the switch.

The propeller caught his necktie, and the blades slowed as the tie wrapped tighter around his neck. "That's it," he croaked. "Exactly."

Steadfast Faith
(Gendusa-Yokum)

As the sun starts sinking each Friday evening, a <u>myriad</u> of villagers, half-starved and <u>slovenly</u> dressed, yet <u>recalcitrant</u>, start streaming down rugged hillsides, determined to demonstrate their faith.

As they approach a makeshift wooden altar, they reach out to dip their fingers into the <u>libation</u>, touching the substance to their foreheads and those of their children.

With firm resolve, they trudge back to their primitive dwellings. Whispers of <u>revolution</u> keep spirits high.

Then one evening, rescue forces overcome the armed camp. Shouts echo through the hills, "We're free! We can go home again. Our prayers are answered!"

Now You Try!
(slovenly, revolution, myriad, libations, recalcitrant)

_____

_____

_____

_____

_____

_____

_____

_____

_____

_____

_____

_____

_____

_____

_____

_____

_____

_____

_____

_____

_____

_____

_____

_____

_____

_____

#19 Flash Tales

(steam, popcorn, fern, recliner, barnacle, suede)

Epiphany
(Neal)

Horace stretched out in his <u>recliner</u>, balancing a bowl of <u>popcorn</u> on his paunch.

<u>Fern</u> washed the supper dishes, then rubbed the <u>steam</u> off the window, and said, "Mother's coming up the drive."

Horace heard the door creak. Suddenly, his mother-in-law was upon him. She stood in her broadcast mode—feet spread apart and hands on hips.

She fired her first volley. "I bought that <u>suede</u> chair for Fern, but here you are—stuck to it like a <u>barnacle</u>." Snap! Big, white bloomers fell down around her ankles. She grabbed them and fled.

"There really is a God," said Horace.

Chaos
(Sagan)

Fred and Thelma relaxed in matching <u>suede</u> <u>recliners</u>. <u>Steam</u> rose from a bowl of fresh <u>popcorn</u> on the table between them.

They smiled contentedly at each other. As they watched a favorite movie, he reached for her hand, but noticed Thelma looking wide-eyed at <u>Barnacle</u>, the cat, racing around the room in erratic pursuit of a fat gray mouse.

"Ah-h-h!" Thelma screamed. She pulled her feet up and perched on top of the chair.

Fred jumped up and knocked over the <u>fern</u>. He landed face down, nose to nose with the mouse.

Barnacle pounced and captured his prey.

Suede
(Raker)

<u>Fern</u> munched <u>popcorn</u> in her new <u>recliner</u>. She had gotten really <u>steamed</u> when Geoffrey called her a slug, but felt better now.

When she'd quit applying for jobs, he got mad. He worked hard, long hours, made good money. Why should she work?

Then he'd fired the housekeeper, pressuring Fern to take over, but no. Seeing her underwear in the entry hall, he yelled, "You <u>barnacle</u>."

Perhaps she'd overreacted. And it had been difficult to achieve her goal. But she was content. The pale <u>suede</u> was quite comfortable, and the birthmark on the armrest would always remind her of Geoffrey.

Bud's Bungled Burglary
(Sikes)

Bud pulled the <u>suede</u> hood over his face. Everything went black. He cursed.

After all the time Ellie took makin' this thing, even <u>steam</u> pressin' it, you'da thought she'da got the eyes straight.

Bud slithered through the window and immediately stumbled over a <u>recliner</u>. As he fell, he grabbed its handle. The footrest popped up and slammed into his jaw. A growling fur ball attached itself to his pants like a <u>barnacle</u>. He kicked, knocking over a table. A bowl of <u>popcorn</u> and a potted <u>fern</u> landed in his lap.

A light came on. A voice roared, "Good boy, Felipe."

Popping Hopping Stopping
Gendusa-Yokum

"Johnny, let's have some <u>popcorn</u> while we watch *Home Alone*. Can you get the popper off that top shelf? I can't reach it," said Peg.

"Yeah, that would be fun. I'll get the bowls ready. I like lots of butter."

Unexpectedly, kernels exploding loosened the lid, sending popcorn everywhere. Hot <u>steam</u> poured forth furiously. Leaping over her <u>recliner</u> to take the pot off the stove, Peg splatted flat down on the slippery floor. Tripping over the potted <u>fern</u> was bad enough, but what really upset her was the hot, buttery popcorn sticking like <u>barnacles</u> on her new red <u>suede</u> shoes.

Now You Try!
(steam, popcorn, fern, recliner, barnacle, suede)

_____

_____

_____

_____

_____

_____

_____

_____

_____

_____

_____

_____

_____

_____

_____

_____

_____

_____

_____

_____

_____

_____

_____

_____

_____

_____

_____

#20 Flash Tales
(bayou, technique, dictionary, example, rationalize)

Sport of Kings
(Neal)

Mavis waited for Edgar to return from the racetrack. Now there is an <u>example</u> of arrested development for you, she thought. The <u>dictionary</u> she had bought him for Father's Day in hopes of raising his consciousness a bit lay gathering dust while he taught their son Carl the <u>technique</u> of picking a winning horse.

The screen door banged, and Edgar rushed in—his face flushed in victory—with Carl following close behind. "Dinner's on me at Bayou Bob's. My horse came in at twenty-to-one."

"What's his name?"

"<u>Rationalize</u>," Edgar said with a grin.

Unjust Restoration
(Sagan)

Two years after the devastating hurricane, little restoration took place on the <u>bayou</u>. Relief agencies <u>rationalized</u> limited aid with excuses of more pressing financial demands. For Glenda's family, this represented another <u>example</u> of inequality. They lost everything but a few clothes and a <u>dictionary</u>. Wealthy areas flourished again. Businesses received prioritized funding. No one seemed to care about Glenda and her neighbors. Hope disappeared. Not knowing anything else to do, she developed her weaving <u>technique</u> and got a job in Louisville. Her family could begin again in a new place, forced to leave the old life behind.

Technique
(Raker)

Pierre thoroughly researched before he began the project. He looked up several terms in the <u>dictionary</u>. He checked reference books for <u>technique</u>. Two of his favorite novels included excellent <u>examples</u>. But everything that seemed appropriate required complicated equipment, scientific knowledge, or physical prowess—which he lacked.

Even as he hitched the trailer to his pickup, Pierre realized he was <u>rationalizing</u>, but it seemed much easier this way.

He carried Marie up the little ladder onto the powerboat. Moonlight illuminated the highway. At the river, he launched and motored off. Finally he stopped, and into the <u>bayou</u>, he dumped her body.

Lanae's Ghost
(Sikes)

Moonlight blanketed the moss-draped cypress and danced on the waters.

"This is an <u>example</u> of your insanity," Christine declared.

"Sh-h-h, or the <u>Bayou</u> Ghost won't come," Lanae whispered.

Christine lowered her voice, "There's no way you can <u>rationalize</u> what we're doing."

"Look!"

A silvery apparition appeared. It floated, dipped, and swayed.

"See?" Lanae whispered. "Exactly what the <u>dictionary</u> says about ghosts. Remember, you must whisper 'I believe' three times."

"Nonsense," Christine said.

Lanae closed her eyes and chanted, "I believe."

When she opened her eyes, Christine had vanished.

Lanae groaned. "Oh, no. She didn't use the right <u>technique</u>."

Vocabulary Homework
(Gendusa-Yokum)

"Tommy, let's review your vocabulary words. I'll call them out, and you write them as <u>examples</u> in sentences."

"Mom, why can't I just say the answers? I hurt my

hand in baseball today."

"Tommy, you are <u>rationalizing</u> because you don't want to do this. Your midterm exam is next week. Two <u>techniques</u> being tested are comprehension and writing skills."

"Okay, hurry. My friends are waiting."

"'<u>Bayou</u>.' Write a sentence using 'bayou.' Then read it out loud."

"Dad promised, 'If you cut the grass for a month, I'll bayou that Spider-Man game.'"

"Tommy, the word is 'bayou.' Please use the <u>dictionary</u>."

Now You Try!
(bayou, technique, dictionary, example, rationalize)

_____
_____
_____
_____
_____
_____
_____
_____
_____
_____
_____
_____
_____
_____
_____
_____
_____
_____
_____
_____
_____
_____
_____
_____
_____
_____
_____
_____
_____

Words Used to Create the Flash Tales

1. lantern, fur, cabbage, embellish, scratch
2. spine, jute, exfoliate, travel, ocean, battery
3. stagger, gastric, turkey, diamond, chimney
4. reprehensible, malevolent, chip, delicacy, unforgiving
5. recipe, humble, providence, mop, basin
6. ingenuous, pernicious, cataclysm, modulate, stockings
7. pennant, ambassador, frenzy, wither, fabric
8. barren, masterful, pique, gardenia, malarkey
9. omit, star, irascible, bricks, rectitude
10. education, deliberate, bumptious, literature, fragile
11. hypnotic, chartreuse, accent, lock, flower
12. deck, chicanery, rapier, cricket, button(s)
13. nebbish, grapes, cup, minimal, chortle, sunset
14. abbreviated, screamed, mud, vaporize, daughter
15. critical, cap, changeling, confused, generous
16. aggregate, conservation, bones, harbor, conducive
17. raucous, canyon, stately, granite, electrifying
18. slovenly, revolution, myriad, libation, recalcitrant
19. steam, popcorn, fern, recliner, barnacle, suede
20. bayou, technique, dictionary, example, rationalize
21. thinker, geranium, bubbles, gravel, bridge

Glossary for Flash Tales

(other possible titles—lexicon, vocabulary, vocabulary builder, word index, "most esoteric word list")

Story #   Word   Definition

1. embellish—*v.t.* **1.** to beautify by or as if by ornamentation; ornament; adorn. **2.** to enhance (a statement or narrative) with fictitious additions.

2. exfoliate—*v.i.* **1.** (of a material) to come apart or be shed from a surface in scales or layers. *v.t.* **2.** to cause to do this. **3.** to wash or rub (a part of the body) with a granular substance to remove dead cells from the surface of the skin.

4. reprehensible—*adj.* deserving censure or condemnation.

4. malevolent—*adj.* having or showing a wish to do evil to others.

5. providence—*n.* **1.** the protective care of God or of nature as a spiritual power. **2.** (cap.) God or nature as providing such care.

6. ingenuous—*adj.* (of a person or action) innocent and unsuspecting.

6. pernicious—*adj.* having a harmful effect, esp. in a gradual or subtle way.

6. cataclysm—*n.* **1.** a large-scale and violent event in the natural world. **2.** a sudden violent upheaval, esp. in a political or social context.

6. modulate—*v.t.* **1.** to exert a modifying or controlling influence on. **2.** to vary the strength, tone, or pitch of (one's voice).

8. pique—*n.* **1.** a feeling of irritation or resentment resulting from a slight, esp. to one's pride. *v.t.* **2.** to stimulate (interest or curiosity). **3. (be piqued)** to feel irritated or resentful.

8. malarkey—*n. Informal.* meaningless talk; nonsense.

9. irascible—*adj.* **1.** (of a person) easily made angry. **2.** characterized by or arising from anger.

9. rectitude—*n. Formal.* morally correct behavior or thinking; righteousness.

10. bumptious—*adj.* self-assertive or proud to an irritating degree.

12. chicanery—*n.* the use of trickery to achieve a political, financial, or legal purpose.

12. rapier—*n.* **1.** a thin, light, sharp-pointed sword used for thrusting. **2.** [as adj.] (especially of speech or intelligence) quick and incisive.

13. nebbish—*n. Informal.* a pitifully ineffectual, luckless, and timid person.

13. chortle—*v.i.* **1.** to chuckle gleefully. *v.t.* **2.** to express with a gleeful chuckle. *n.* **3.** a gleeful chuckle.

15. changeling—*n.* a child believed to have been secretly substituted by fairies for the parents' real child in infancy.

16. aggregate—*adj.* **1.** formed by the conjunction or collection of particulars into a whole mass or sum; total; combined. *n.* **2.** a sum, mass, or assemblage of particulars; a total or gross amount. **3.** a cluster of soil granules not larger than a small crumb. **4.** any of various loose, particulate materials, as sand, gravel, or pebbles, added to a cementing agent to make concrete, plaster, etc. *v.t.* **5.** to bring together, collect into one sum, mass, or body. *v.i.* **6.** to combine and form a collection or mass.

16. conducive—*adj.* making a certain situation or outcome likely or possible.

17. raucous—*adj.* making or constituting a disturbingly harsh and loud noise.

18. slovenly—*adj.* **1.** (esp. of a person or their appearance) messy and dirty. **2.** (esp. of a person or action) careless; excessively casual.

18. myriad—*n.* **1.** a very great or infinitely great number of persons or things. *adj.* **2**. of an infinitely great number; innumerable. **3**. having innumerable phases, aspects, variations, etc.

18. libation—*n.* **1**. a drink poured out as an offering to a deity. **2**. the pouring out of such a drink-offering. **3**. *Humorous.* a drink.

18. recalcitrant—*adj.* **1**. resisting authority or control; not obedient or compliant. **2**. hard to deal with, manage, or operate. *n.* **3**. a recalcitrant person.

19. barnacle—*n.* **1**. a marine crustacean (class Cirripedia) with an external shell, which attaches itself permanently to a variety of surfaces. **2**. a person or thing that clings tenaciously.

22. reminisce—*v.i.* indulge in enjoyable recollection of past events.

23. existentialism—*n.* a philosophical theory or approach that emphasizes the existence of the individual person as a free and responsible agent determining his or her own development through acts of the will.

23. surmount—*v.t.* **1**. overcome (a difficulty or obstacle). **2**. (usu. **be surmounted**) stand or be placed on top of.

24. gossamer—*n.* **1**. a fine, filmy substance consisting of cobwebs spun by small spiders, which is seen esp. in autumn. **2.** something extremely light, flimsy, or delicate. *adj.* **3.** made of or resembling gossamer.

25. libel—*n.* **1.** *Law* **a.** a published false statement that is damaging to a person's reputation; a written defamation. **b.** the action or crime of publishing such a statement. **c.** a false and malicious statement about a person. *v.t.* **3.** *Law* **a.** defame (someone) by publishing a libel. **b.** make a false and malicious statement about.

26. juxtaposition—*n.* **1.** an act or instance of placing close together or side by side, esp. for comparison or contrast. **2.** the state of being close together or side by side.

26. filigree—*n.* **1.** delicate ornamental work of fine silver, gold, or other metal wires, esp. lacy jewelers' work of scrolls and arabesques. **2.** anything very delicate or fanciful. *adj.* **3.** composed of or resembling filigree. *v.t.* **4.** to adorn with or form into filigree.

26. tinker—*n.* **1. a.**(esp. in former times) a person who travels from place to place mending pans, kettles, and other metal utensils as a way of making a living. **b.** a person who makes minor mechanical repairs, esp. on a variety of appliances and apparatuses, usually for a living. **c.** *Brit., chiefly derogatory.* a gypsy or other person living in an itinerant community. **2.** an act of attempting to repair something. *v.i.* **3.** to attempt to repair or improve something in a casual or desultory way, often to no useful effect. *v.t.* **4.** *Archaic* to attempt to mend (something) in such a way.

27. murky—*adj.* **1.** dark, gloomy, and cheerless. **2.** obscure or thick with mist, haze, etc., as the air. **3.** vague, confused, unclear.

27. taciturn—*adj.* (of a person) reserved or uncommunicative in speech; saying little.

28. visceral—*adj.* **1.** of or pertaining to the viscera (the internal organs in the abdomen). **2.** relating to deep inward feelings rather than to the intellect.

28. latent—*adj.* **1.** (of a quality or state) existing but not yet developed or manifest; hidden; concealed. *Biol.* **2.** (of a bud, resting stage, etc.) lying dormant or hidden until circumstances are suitable for development or manifestation. **3.** (of a disease) in which the usual symptoms are not yet manifest. **4.** (of a microorganism, esp. a virus) present in the body without causing disease, but capable of doing so at a later stage or when transmitted to another body.

29. fretful—*adj.* feeling or expressing distress or irritation.

29. cacophony—*n.* a harsh, discordant mixture of sounds.

29. persiflage—*n.* light and slightly contemptuous mockery or banter.

32. capitulate—*v.i.* to cease to resist an opponent or an unwelcome demand; to surrender.

33. churlish—*adj.* rude in a mean-spirited and surly way.

34. livercheese—*n.* a specialty food found in southern Germany, similar to bologna sausage.

34. mercurial—*adj.* **1.** (of a person) subject to sudden or unpredictable changes; (of a person) sprightly; lively. **2.** of or containing the element mercury. **3. (Mercurial)** of the planet Mercury. *n.* **4.** (usu. **mercurials**) a drug or other compound containing mercury.

38. talisman—*n.* an object, typically an inscribed ring or stone, that is thought to have magic powers and to bring good luck.

40. cauterize—*v.t. Medicine to* burn the skin or flesh of (a wound) with a heated instrument or caustic substance, typically to stop bleeding or prevent the wound from becoming infected.

40. moussaka—*n.* a Greek dish made of minced lamb, eggplant, and tomatoes, with cheese on top.

To order additional copies of *Flash Tales*
and other books by talented *WordWright* authors

Name _____

Address _____

_____

_____

Flash Tales
        by Sikes, Neal, Raker, Sagan, Gendusa-Yokum
$9.95 x _____ copies = _____

Other books from WordWright
WordWright LX

Shelter from the Storm
        by Dianne G. Sagan
$14.95 x _____ copies = _____

The Legend of Dragon Sword
        by Ellen Newton Driscoll
$14.95 x _____ copies = _____

The Haunting of Candlewood
        by Ellen Newton Driscoll
$14.95 x _____ copies = _____

The Dragons of Candlewood
         by Ellen Newton Driscoll
$14.95 x _____ copies = _____

The Drums of Gerald Hurd: A Supernatural Mystery
         by L.C. Hayden
$14.95 x _____ copies = _____

A Serpent's Tooth
         by Joan R. Neubauer
$18.95 x _____ copies = _____

The Ballad of Ol' Hook
         by Tom Townsend
$14.95 x _____ copies = _____

Shadow Dancing
         by Joan R. Neubauer and Stephen F. Neubauer
$14.95 x _____ copies = _____

Collect all the fine books from WordWright

One Night Books

#1 — *Ghosts of Whitner*
         by Jean LeVitt
$9.95 x _____ copies = _____

#2 — *Upsizing Your Career*
       by Marty Morris
$9.95 x _____ copies = _____

#3 — *Special Delivery*
       by Joan R. Neubauer and Stephen F. Neubauer
$9.95 x _____ copies = _____

#4 — *Dark Tales of the Tower*
       by Donna Munch
$9.95 x _____ copies = _____

#5 — *Shortcuts to Happiness:*
       Simple Things Happy People Do
       by Bob Sutherland
$9.95 x _____ copies = _____

#6 — *Rheumatoid Arthritis: The Alternate Route*
       by Suzanne Harris, PhD.
$9.95 x _____ copies = _____

#7 — *Syncopated Summer*
       by Barbara Rollins
$9.95 x _____ copies = _____

#8 — *Notorious Nora*
　　　by Kelly Jones
$9.95 (paperback) x _____ copies = _____
$19.95 (casebound) x_____ copies = _____

The Adventure Tree by Kelly Jones
$13.99 (paperback) x _____ copies = _____
$19.99 (casebound) x _____ copies =_____

The Adventure Tree – Branch II by Kelly Jones
A Royal Magic Show
$13.99 (paperback) x _____ copies = _____
$19.99 (casebound) x _____ copies =_____

The Adventure Tree – Branch III by Kelly Jones
A Crystal Clear Christmas
$13.99 (paperback) x _____ copies = _____
$19.99 (casebound) x _____ copies =_____

#9 — *Sammie*
　　　by Barbara Newton
$9.95 x _____ copies = _____

#10—*Inventing Chloe*
　　　by JoAn Watson Martin
$9.95 x _____ copies = _____

\#11—*The Hail and the Fury*
     by Gordon Payne
$9.95 x _____ copies = _____

Sales Tax _____
(Texas residents add 8.25% sales tax)

Please add $3.00 postage and handling for the first book
and $1.25 for each additional book

_____

Total amount due: _____

Please send check or money order for books to:
WordWright.biz, Inc.
WordWright Business Park
46561 State Highway 118
Alpine, Texas 79830

We also invite you to call 877/380-3321,
our toll free number,
and order by credit card.

For a complete catalog of books,
visit our sites at
http://www.WordWright.biz
and
SpecialDeliveryBooks.com

LaVergne, TN USA
10 December 2009
166537LV00001B/5/P